Kids Nuttiest Jokes

Mike Benny
illustrated by
Sanford Hoffman

Sterling Publishing Co., Inc.
New York

10 9 8 7

Published in 2003 by Sterling Publishing Co., Inc.
387 Park Avenue South, New York, NY 10016
© 1993 by Mike Benny
Originally published in hardcover under the title *World's Punniest Joke Book*
Distributed in Canada by Sterling Publishing
c/o Canadian Manda Group, 165 Dufferin Street
Toronto, Ontario, Canada M6K 3H6
Distributed in Great Britain and Europe by Chris Lloyd at Orca Book
Services, Stanley House, Fleets Lane, Poole BH15 3AJ, England
Distributed in Australia by Capricorn Link (Australia) Pty. Ltd.
P.O. Box 704, Windsor, NSW 2756, Australia

Manufactured in the United States of America

Sterling ISBN 1-4027-0624-3

CONTENTS

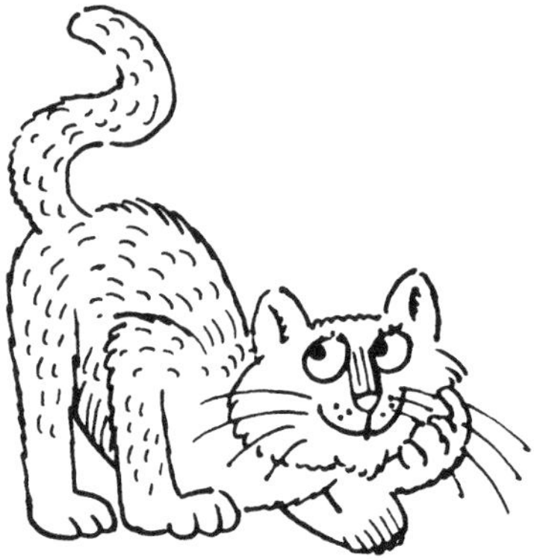

1. SAY IT AIN'T SO!

What did the jellybean say to the Snickers bar?
"Smile, you're on candied camera."

What did the wise old canary say to the parrot?
"Talk is cheap-cheap."

What did one canned mushroom say to the other canned mushroom?
"There's not mushroom (much room) in here."

What did the sock say to the needle?
"I'll be darned!"

What did the scarf say to the hat?
  "You go on ahead, I'll hang around."

What did the nylons say to the garter belt?
  "Make it snappy. I've got a run."

What did the shoe say to the shoelace?
  "Forget me knot."

What did the baked potato say to the cook?
  "Foiled again!"

What did the police say when a famous drawing was stolen?
  "Details are sketchy."

What did the coffee say to the police?
  "I've been mugged."

What did the comedian say to the cattle rancher?

"Herd any good ones lately?"

What did the farmer say when he saw three holes in the ground?

"Well, well, well!"

What did the farmer say when he lost the butter?

"It'll churn up."

What do hens say every morning?

"Snap, cackle, pop."

What do you say to a guy who wrote a book about clock repair?

"It's about time."

What do you say to curtains?

"Pull yourself together."

What do you say to your piano teacher?

"Get off my Bach."

What do you say to a person who wakes up with a black eye?

"Rise and shine-r."

What do you say to a closet?
"Clothes the door."

What did the priest say to the salesman?
"Nun for me."

What did the priest say to the stranger?
"Your faith looks familiar."

What do you say to a stubborn tailor?
"Suit yourself."

What do you say to a nudist?
"Clad to see you."

What do you say to a stubborn chimney sweep?
"Soot yourself."

What do you say to a stubborn lawyer?
"Sue-it yourself."

What do you say to a baby in designer clothes?
"Gucci Gucci goo."

What do you say to a king who falls off his chair?

   "Throne for a loop?"

What do you say to a guy driving a car with no engine?

   "How's it going?"

What do you say to an annoying car mechanic?

   "Give me a brake (break)."

What do you say to introduce a hamburger?

   "Meat Patty."

What do you say to a boomerang on its birthday?

   "Many happy returns."

2. WHY OH WHY?

Why did the undertaker write a book?
He had a good plot.

Why was the undertaker so nervous putting on a play?
He didn't have time to re-hearse.

Why did the cottage go on a diet?
It wanted to be a lighthouse.

Why did the sailor jump rope?
He hoped he'd become the skipper.

Why didn't the skeleton cross the road?
It didn't have the guts.

Why did the ghost apologize?
It spook out of turn.

Why did the dynamite always get what it wanted?
No one could re-fuse it.

Why didn't the kitchen window like the living-room window?
Because it was such a big pain (pane).

Why was the dumbbell late?
It got held up at the gym.

Why did the cow jump over the moon?
To make a milky way.

Why was the plumber so tired?
He felt drained.

Why did the plumber start dancing?
He knew a little tap.

Why didn't the elephant buy a Porsche?
It had no trunk space.

Why did the garbage collector go on a diet?
He was worried about his waste-line (waistline).

Why did the pinky go to jail?
He was fingered by the police.

Why does it take so long to make a politician-snowman?
You have to hollow out the head first.

Why do gamblers love Ireland?
They keep Dublin their odds.

Why didn't the weatherman ever get tired?
He always got a second wind.

Why didn't the weatherman call for more wind?
He thought it was dis-gusting.

Why did the farmer take two aspirins before going to the cornfield?
In case he got an ear-acre (acher).

Why did the carpenter break all his teeth?
From chewing his nails.

Why did the silly kid take a whip and chair to the Improv?
He heard the jokers were wild.

Why do nuns watch soap operas?
They get into the habit.

3. DID YOU HEAR...?

Did you hear about the street vendor who sold pudding?

It was custard's (Custer's) last stand.

Did you hear about the helpful policeman?

He was on the ad-vice squad.

Did you hear about the model at the debate?

She posed a good question.

Did you hear the joke about the mountain climber?

He hasn't made it up yet.

Did you hear about the sword swallower who worked for nothing?

He was a free-lancer.

Did you hear about the musician who was upset?

He couldn't compose himself.

Did you hear about the absent-minded musician?

He finally left himself notes.

Did you hear about the artist with a poor memory?

He kept drawing a blank.

Did you hear about the cabdriver who was fired?

He was driving customers away.

Did you hear about the kid who was twenty minutes early for school?

He was in a class by himself.

Did you hear about the kid who didn't like something about school?

It was the principal of the thing.

Weather or Not

Did you hear about the weatherman who went back to college?

He got several degrees.

Did you hear about the weatherman who won the race?

He said it was a breeze.

Did you hear about the world's best weatherman?

He's the raining (reigning) champion.

Did you hear about the actors in the paper-towel commercial?

There were four rolls (roles).

Did you hear about the cattle rancher at the poker game?

He kept raising the steaks.

Did you hear about the cowboy in the leaves?

He was accused of rustling.

Did you hear about the couple married in a bathtub?

They wanted a double ring ceremony.

Did you hear about the glue truck that overturned?

Police were asking motorists to stick to their own lanes.

Did you hear about the nudist runner?

He could do the hundred yard dash in nothing.

Did you hear about the soldier who wanted to be a pastry chef?

He was a desserter (deserter).

Did you hear about the deck chair factories that lost money?

They folded.

Did you hear about the accident at the soup factory?

Two workers got canned.

Did you hear about the job at the coffee-maker factory?

It doesn't pay much, but there are lots of perks.

Did you hear about the nearsighted logger?

What he couldn't see the chain saw.

Did you hear about the 30-year-old butcher?

He was in his prime.

Balmy in the Army

Did you hear about the investigator who joined the army?

He was a private eye.

Did you hear about the doctor who joined the army?

He was a general practitioner.

Did you hear about the umpire who joined the army?

He moved from base to base.

Did you hear about the absent-minded train conductor?

He lost track of things.

Did you hear about the school bus that had to repeat a grade?

Its brakes failed.

Did you hear about the class bully who was thrown out of the library?

He was hitting the books too hard.

Did you hear about the boarding house that blew up?

Rumors (roomers) were flying.

Did you hear the story about the bed?

It was just made up.

Did you hear about the street-corner artist?

He had no trouble drawing a large crowd.

Did you hear about the farmer who wrote dirty letters?

He used a pig pen.

Did you hear about the guy who brought his fishing lures back to shore?

He wanted a re-bait.

Did you hear about the fish that got a face-lift?

He went to a plastic sturgeon.

Did you hear about the knitting needle that told jokes?

It could keep you in stitches.

4. ALL WORK & NO PLAY

What do you call an aged tailor?
An old sew-and-sew.

What's the hardest part of an astronaut's job?
Washing the (satellite) dishes.

LARRY: I tried to get a job at a hotel.
BARRY: What happened?
LARRY: They were looking for someone who was INN-experienced.

How is the astronomer doing?
Things are looking up.

How is the archaeologist doing?
Her life's work is in ruins.

What do you get when you cross a boxer and a photographer?
A striking resemblance.

NED: My brother is in the candy business.
TED: Is he doing well?
NED: So far he's made a mint.

Why did they go on strike at the mint?
They were making too much money.

Why did the secretary take a bikini to work?
She heard she would go in the typing pool.

WIT: I lost my job writing obituaries.
NIT: What happened?
WIT: I missed a deadline.

How do you fire a mailman?
Give him the sack.

Why would you go to the art gallery for a job?
They usually have a few openings.

MART: How is the monogram business?
DART: I've had some initial success.

What does the bicycle salesman do with bikes?
He peddles (pedals) them.

How do you find a writer in a crowded building?
Have him paged.

What happened to the novelist who was arrested?
He was printed and booked.

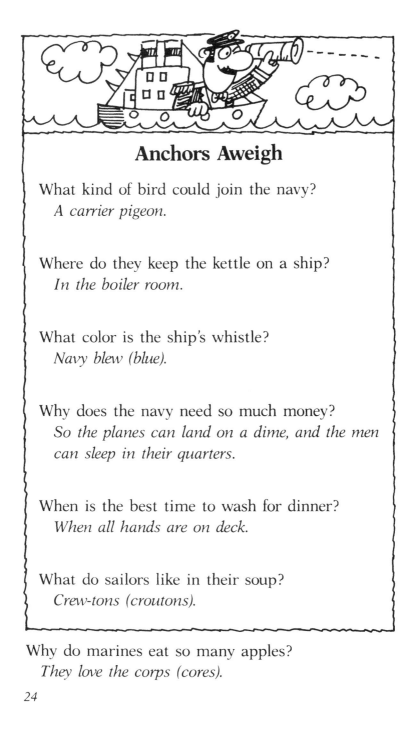

Anchors Aweigh

What kind of bird could join the navy?
A carrier pigeon.

Where do they keep the kettle on a ship?
In the boiler room.

What color is the ship's whistle?
Navy blew (blue).

Why does the navy need so much money?
So the planes can land on a dime, and the men can sleep in their quarters.

When is the best time to wash for dinner?
When all hands are on deck.

What do sailors like in their soup?
Crew-tons (croutons).

Why do marines eat so many apples?
They love the corps (cores).

Army or Aren't We?

Where does the army hide its garbage?
In the mess tent.

What does the army do with priests?
It sends them on secret missions.

Where does the army keep its furs?
In fox-holes.

Where did they put the psychic who joined the army?
On a trance-port (transport) ship.

Why did the two plumbers work together?
They were in sync (sink).

Why did the plumber decide to get married?
It was time he took the plunge-r.

What does it take to be a plumber?
Pipe dreams.

Why did the weatherman measure the thermometer?
Because he wanted to know the fahren-height.

How did the weatherman get to work?
He hailed a cab.

Why was the mechanic in trouble?
For leaving oily (early).

How did the mechanic hear a secret?
The tires squealed.

What kind of ties do barbers wear?
Clip-ons.

What did the botanist say to the pine forest?
"Don't ever leave."

Why did the waiter fall over?
 He was tipped.

Where do jewellers go on vacation?
 On sapphire-i (safari).

Did you hear about the gardener who planted a telephone?
 They gave him a ring-around-the-rosies.

What do you call the boss at a lumberyard?
 The chairman of the boards.

How could you tell the tailor was tired?
 He was panting.

How could you tell the dressmaker was healthy?
 She seamed (seemed) well.

What superhero works at the supermarket?
 Clerk Kent.

What do you give a retired bus driver?
 A token of appreciation.

What did the bus driver do with the thief?
 Let him off.

5. SHOP TILL YOU DROP

How do you buy a hammer?
By the pound.

How do you buy a house?
By the yard.

How do you buy grandparents?
By the gram.

How do you buy a bed?
By the sack.

How do you buy a detective?
By the case.

How do you buy men's socks?
Through the male (mail).

How do you buy a thief?
On the Home Shoplifting Channel.

How do you buy No-Name items?
Anonymously.

Where do you buy doors?
At a dor-mitory.

Where do you buy a mink coat?
At a fur-niture store.

Where do electricians buy supplies?
At a factory outlet.

Where do you buy a comb?
At a parts store.

How does a little oven say hello?
With a micro-wave.

What kind of game can you play at a shopping center?
Price tag.

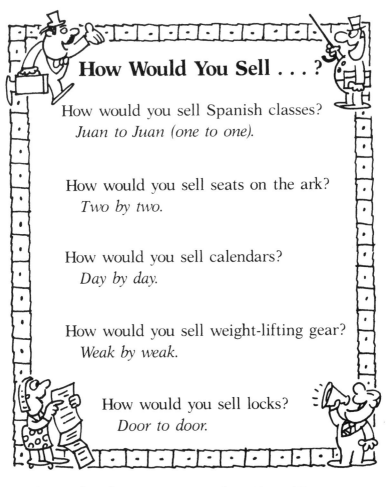

How Would You Sell . . . ?

How would you sell Spanish classes?
Juan to Juan (one to one).

How would you sell seats on the ark?
Two by two.

How would you sell calendars?
Day by day.

How would you sell weight-lifting gear?
Weak by weak.

How would you sell locks?
Door to door.

Why is the shopping so good in Hawaii?
There are isle after isle of savings.

Why is the shopping so good in Mexico?
You only peso (pay-so) much.

Why didn't the actor like shopping?
There weren't enough lines.

What was the biologist doing at the store?
He was looking for new genes (jeans).

Why did the biologist get a job at the store?
He really knew how to cell (sell).

What happened to the fighter at the shopping center?
He was malled (mauled).

How did the ex-convict get a job at the music store?
They found out he had a record.

Where do police shop?
At the department store.

Where would you get your taxes done?
At the Returns department.

What do you call a dog at the stereo shop?
  A woofer.

What do you call a little bird at the stereo shop?
  A tweeter.

How did the dove save so much money?
  By using coooo-pons (coupons).

Why would you shop for a car in Las Vegas?
  They have so many dealers.

What did the duck say to the clerk?
  "Put this on my bill."

Why was the encyclopedia salesman so quiet?
Someone turned down the volume.

Why was the baseball player at the store?
For a sales pitch.

Why was the lifeguard at the store?
He heard he could save a lot.

Why was the fruit stand empty?
It hadn't been re-peared (repaired).

What do you call a hockey player in a store?
A shopping center.

At the store, what do you say after they say "hello"?
"Good buy."

6. SCHOOL DAYS

Did you hear about the witch who was kicked out of school?
She was ex-spelled (expelled).

What did Colonel Sanders learn in school?
The twelve secret verbs and spices.

How do you find a math tutor?
Place an add (ad).

Did you hear about the successful school play?
It was a class act.

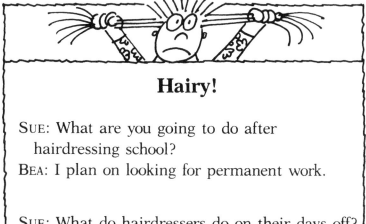

Hairy!

Sue: What are you going to do after
  hairdressing school?
Bea: I plan on looking for permanent work.

Sue: What do hairdressers do on their days off?
Bea: Curl up with a good book.

What happened when the banker missed a day
of school?
  He brought a note.

Why did you need a reservation at the library?
  It was booked-up.

Did you hear about the pitcher at school?
  He was graded on a curve.

Why did the historian read books on the ancient
Greeks?
  It was his favorite past-time.

How do astrologers talk to each other?
  In sign language.

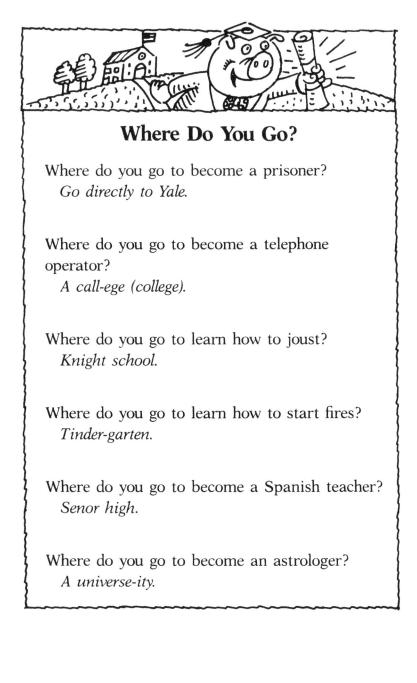

Where Do You Go?

Where do you go to become a prisoner?
Go directly to Yale.

Where do you go to become a telephone operator?
A call-ege (college).

Where do you go to learn how to joust?
Knight school.

Where do you go to learn how to start fires?
Tinder-garten.

Where do you go to become a Spanish teacher?
Senor high.

Where do you go to become an astrologer?
A universe-ity.

7. THE ZANY ZOO

What swims and has six pockets?
A pool shark.

Why were the wildebeests so happy?
They heard there would be no gnu hunters.

What is striped and then spotted?
A zebra that's been seen.

What is both large and small at the same time?
A jumbo shrimp.

How much did the polar bear weigh?
  A ton-*dra (tundra).*

What do you call a parrot in a raincoat?
  Polly-unsaturated.

What kind of fisherman always cries?
  A *whaler (wailer).*

What do you say to a crying whale?
  "Quit your blubbering."

How does a whale walk?
  Eel toe, eel toe, eel toe.

Hop To It

Did you hear about the quiet frog?
He never said a word till the day he croaked.

When is a car like a frog?
When it's being toad.

What happens if you swallow a frog?
You could croak at any minute.

What do you get when you cross Moby Dick and a Timex?
A whale watch-er.

Why was the tuna so sad when he lost his wife?
He lobster, and couldn't flounder.

What do you call 300 rabbits marching backwards?
A receding hare line.

Did you hear about the sleepy king of the beasts?

He was lion down.

Who cuts the lion's hair?

His mane man.

SOD: I tried to make an elephant fly.
TOD: Could you do it?
SOD: No. I couldn't find a long enough zipper.

What do you call a fly with no wings?

A walk.

What do you call a deer with no eyes?

No-eye deer.

Why did the seal cross the road?

To get to the otter side.

Why did the bird like to sit down?

He was a stool pigeon.

How could you tell the bird liked his home?

He wouldn't stop raven about it.

8. YOUNG MACDONALD'S FARM

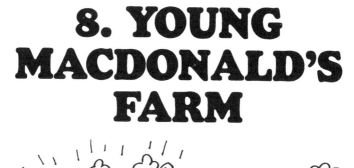

Did you hear about the cow that couldn't give milk?

She thought she was an udder failure.

What did the cow say to the bull in the car?

"I'll drive, you steer."

What is the cow's favorite song?

"Moooo-n River."

What is the potato's favorite song?

"I Only Have Eyes for You."

Chicken Feed

How much do they pay chickens for their eggs?
A poultry (paltry) sum.

Why do chickens need vacations?
They get cooped up all day.

Why do roosters crow?
Because crows roost.

What did the farmer say when he saw three ducks in his mailbox?
"Bills, bills, bills."

Are potatoes good drivers?
When they keep their eyes peeled.

Where do they keep all the pigs in Idaho?
In the state pen.

How do you fix a hole in the garden?
With a vegetable patch.

How do baby sheep stay cool in the summer?
They use a lamb-shade.

Why did the farmer's wife think no one listened
to her?
Only the sheep heard-her (herder).

What do you call a cow that can't do anything
right?
Miss-steak.

What do you say to a sleeping vegetable
gardener?
"Rest in peas."

What do you call a horse that never stops
telling you what to do?
  A real nag.

What was the horse doing at the stock market?
  Bucking the trends.

How can you make a flower say something?
  There are vase to make it s-talk.

What do you call a kitten that cheats on a test?
  A copy cat.

What do you call a sloppy little cat?
  A kitty litterer.

What do you call the man who sprays the flowers?

"Mist-er."

Did you hear about the lawn mower that went on the stage?

It had a scrapbook full of clippings.

What did the blacksmith say to the runaway horse?

"Stop or I'll shoe-it (shoot)."

Did you hear about the corn farmer who joined the army?

He wanted to be a colonel (kernel).

How did the tractor get his son a job on the farm?

He had some pull.

What do you call a fashion-conscious dog?

A trend setter.

What dog is the best flier?

An air-dale.

What kind of dog likes corn on the cob?

A Husk-y.

What would happen if you crossed a pit bull with a yappy poodle?
You'd get a vicious gossip.

What kind of dog likes air conditioning?
A hot dog.

What do you do with a rented dog?
Put him on a lease (leash).

What is the most expensive dog?
A golden retriever.

What kind of shoes do dog trainers wear?
Hush puppies.

DARCY: I got my dog a flea collar.
MARCH: Did he like it?
DARCY: No. It ticked him off.

What did the dog say when someone grabbed his tail?
"That's the end of me!"

9. STARS ON PARADE!

Why did the Hollywood chicken cross the road?
To see Gregory Peck.

What musical group can open any door?
New Kids On The Lock.

Who is Buckwheat's famous brother?
Kareem of wheat.

How can you tell Madonna buys her clothes on sale?

Because they are always half-off.

What do Kermit the Frog and Mack the Knife have in common?

The same middle name.

What do you say when you want Dolly's attention?

"Parton me."

Why didn't the king and queen potato want their daughter to marry the anchorman?

Because he was just a common-tater (commentator).

Silly Cash Stash

Where does Jack Frost keep all his money?
In a slush fund.

How did Old Man River lose all his money?
He got soaked.

Where do kittens get their money from?
Pet-ty cash.

Where does Mother Nature keep her money?
In a cloud bank.

Where does a track star keep his money?
In a pole vault.

How did we find out about the goose that laid
the golden egg?
Both Jack and the beans-talk (beanstalk).

Why didn't Mata Hari ever smile?
She was no laughing Mata.

Did Adam and Eve ever have a date?
No, just an apple.

Where does Snow White keep her yacht?
At any of her seven wharfs (dwarfs).

Where is Captain Hook's treasure chest?
Under his treasure shirt.

What is tasty and a great inventor?
Marconi and Cheese.

Who hasn't done his ironing in years?
Wrinkle Stilskin.

Did you know most of King Arthur's men had
insomnia?
It was one sleepless knight after another.

What does the Lone Ranger's horse eat with?
Silverware.

Why did the three pigs leave home?
Their father was a boar.

Why was Roy Rogers always smiling and shooting his gun?

He was Trigger happy.

Did you know what Mr. Goodyear is doing now?

He is re-tired.

What do you say to a silent movie star?

"You should be scene and not heard."

What did the Mighty Samson do when his son grew a pony tail?

He cut his heir.

Let's Make-Up

How do you glue your mouth shut?
With lipstick.

Who do you call if your lipstick gets sick?
A cos-medic (cosmetic).

What happened to the lady who stole some eye make-up?
She got fifty lashes.

How do they ship cosmetics?
On an eye liner.

Why did the comedian get a job at the beauty shop?
So he could make-up some new ones.

Did you hear about the lady who chewed her nails?
She polished off all of them.

Why can't bad actors fish?
They never remember their lines.

Where does Superman go bowling?
At Lois Lanes.

What happened when Santa took boxing lessons?
He decked the halls.

Who brings gifts to the dentist's office?
Santa Floss.

What's the difference between a knight and Rudolph?
One is a dragon slayer, the other is a sleigh dragger.

Where does Santa keep his suit?
In the Claus-it (closet).

What kind of cars do Santa's elves drive?
Toyotas.

Who sings and helps Santa?
Elves Presley.

Who helps Santa when the elves are busy?
The Twelve Daves of Christmas.

What do you call Santa Claus when he's almost late?
The Saint Nick-of-time.

Where does Saint Nick go on holidays?
Santa Cruz.

Where does Mrs. Claus go on holidays?
Santa Fe.

Did you hear about the invisible Santa?
You can't see him, but you can feel his presents.

10. GAMES PEOPLE PLAY

What game do birds like to play?
Hide and beak.

What game do you play with bees?
Hive and seek.

What game can you play while the earth is shaking?
Quakes and ladders.

What is a baker's favorite game?
Tic Tac Dough.

How did the football player get into the theater for free?

He received a pass.

What did the fisherman take to the football game?

His tackle.

Where does your mother's mother sit at the ballgame?

In the grand-stand.

Why did the boxer change his socks?

He could smell defeat (the feet).

How did the bus driver lose the game?

He missed his turn.

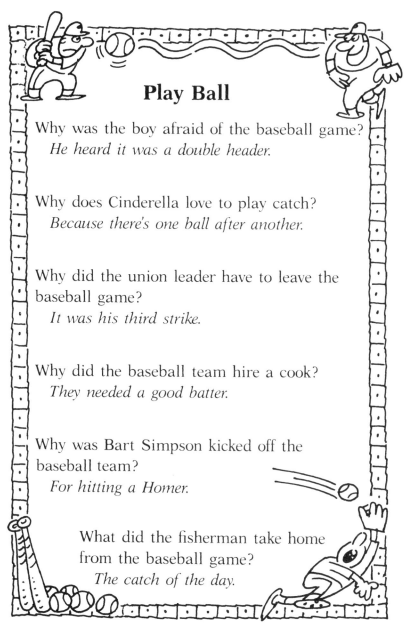

Play Ball

Why was the boy afraid of the baseball game?
He heard it was a double header.

Why does Cinderella love to play catch?
Because there's one ball after another.

Why did the union leader have to leave the
baseball game?
It was his third strike.

Why did the baseball team hire a cook?
They needed a good batter.

Why was Bart Simpson kicked off the
baseball team?
For hitting a Homer.

What did the fisherman take home
from the baseball game?
The catch of the day.

Why did the high jumper check the calendar?
To see if it was a leap year.

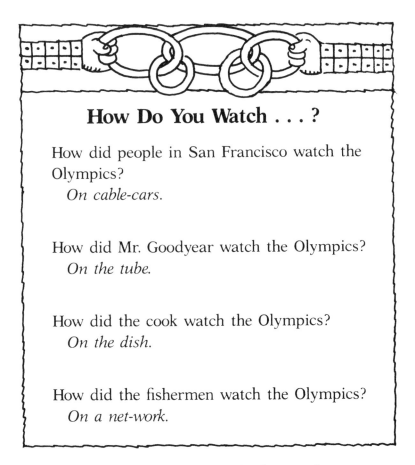

How Do You Watch . . . ?

How did people in San Francisco watch the Olympics?
On cable-cars.

How did Mr. Goodyear watch the Olympics?
On the tube.

How did the cook watch the Olympics?
On the dish.

How did the fishermen watch the Olympics?
On a net-work.

Why did the runner bring his barber to the Olympics?
He wanted to shave a few seconds off his time.

What did the silly swimmer do with his Olympic gold medal?
He had it bronzed.

11. PROS & CONS

What did the artist say in court?
"This painting was framed."

Did you hear about the proud prisoner?
He was taught never to be ashamed of his convictions.

What do bank robbers like with their soup?
Safe crackers.

What kind of telephones do convicts prefer?
Cell-ular phones.

Why did the mob want to kill Einstein?

He knew too much.

Did you hear about the guy who stole the judge's calendar?

He got twelve months.

What did the witch say after the California plane was cancelled?

"There's no west for the wicked."

What did the grateful iceberg say to the *Titanic*?

"Sank you very much."

What did the *Titanic* want from its boss?

A raise.

What is the best thing about being a sick thief?
You can always take something for it.

Did you hear about the shoplifter at the lingerie shop?
She gave police the slip.

Did you hear about the thief at the butcher shop?
He jumped on the scale and gave himself a weigh (away).

Did you hear about the convict who was allergic to jail?
He would break-out in hives.

Did you hear about the short psychic who escaped from jail?
A small medium at large!

Why should you never interrupt a fat judge while he's eating?
There's too much at steak.

How do we know that Al Capone had venetian blinds?
Otherwise it would have been curtains for him.

What kind of lotion do monsters wear at the beach?

Sunscream.

Who wrote the monster's favorite book?

A ghost writer.

What kind of glasses do monsters drink from?

Franken-steins.

How does a werewolf brush its hairy mouth?

With a fine tooth comb.

Why was Doctor Jekyll so hard to find?

He knew how to Hyde.

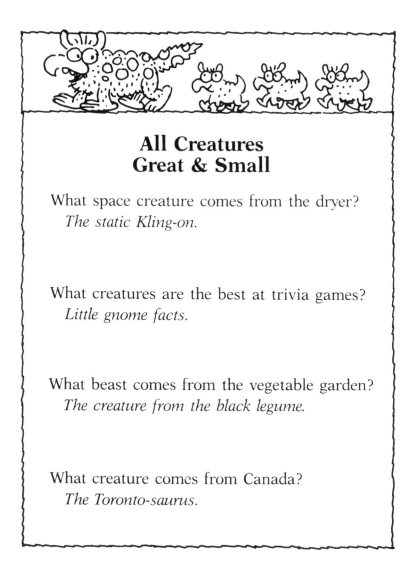

All Creatures Great & Small

What space creature comes from the dryer?
The static Kling-on.

What creatures are the best at trivia games?
Little gnome facts.

What beast comes from the vegetable garden?
The creature from the black legume.

What creature comes from Canada?
The Toronto-saurus.

What did the prisoner say to the judge?
"Pardon me."

How do Eskimos stick together?
With i-glue (igloo).

What happened when the seats in all the police cars were stolen?

Police had nothing to go on.

Why was the weatherman arrested?

For shooting the breeze.

What happened to the guy who stole three hundred O'Henry's?

He ended up behind bars.

Did you hear about the slow composer?

He ended up behind bars too.

What happened to the retired bartender?

He's no longer behind bars.

What prison did they send the canary to?

Sing Sing.

Why was the clock in prison?

It was just doing time.

12. QUICK SNAPPERS

"Atheism is a non-prophet organization."

"Catching a Sasquatch would be a big feat."

"Does the name Pavlov ring a bell?"

"Hopefully, this water is from a wishing well."

"My job at the phone company is really taking its toll."

"Bad spellers untie!"

Wouldn't It Be Funny If . . . ?

A dressmaker slipped.

A logger fell.

A travel agent tripped.

A record skipped town.

A fisherman saw Annette (a net).

A painter got new shades.

A surfer waved.

An onion leaked.

A dentist had a fire drill.

A golfer joined a club.

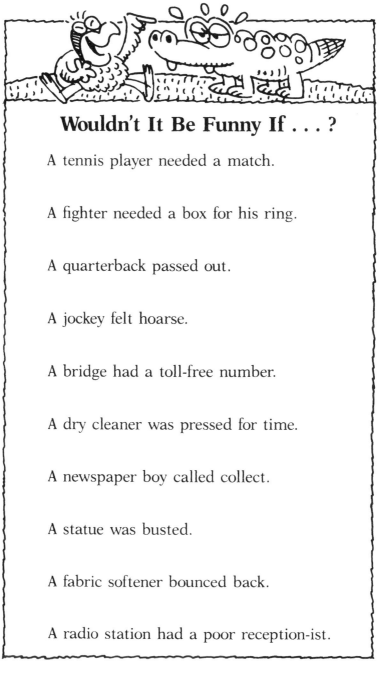

Wouldn't It Be Funny If . . . ?

A tennis player needed a match.

A fighter needed a box for his ring.

A quarterback passed out.

A jockey felt hoarse.

A bridge had a toll-free number.

A dry cleaner was pressed for time.

A newspaper boy called collect.

A statue was busted.

A fabric softener bounced back.

A radio station had a poor reception-ist.

The Doubtful Dictionary

Naval Destroyer:
A hula hoop with a nail in it.

Penmanship:
What writers use to cross the ocean.

Writer's block:
Where all the writers live.

Wine glasses:
What near-sighted complainers wear.

Silver screen:
What rich sunbathers wear.

Bacteria:
The far end of a cafeteria.

Did you hear about the human cannonball who couldn't be fired?

Did you hear about the human cannonball who was lost?
It was tough to find a man of his caliber.

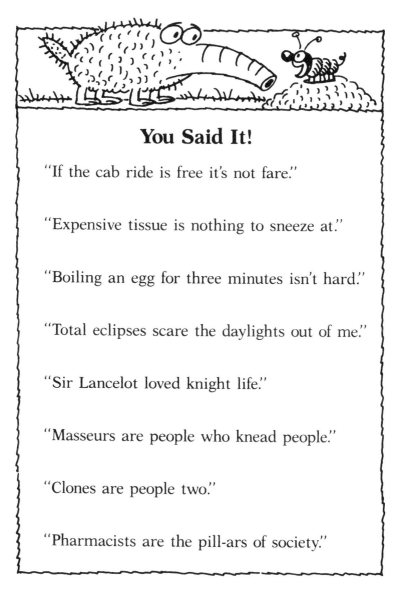

You Said It!

"If the cab ride is free it's not fare."

"Expensive tissue is nothing to sneeze at."

"Boiling an egg for three minutes isn't hard."

"Total eclipses scare the daylights out of me."

"Sir Lancelot loved knight life."

"Masseurs are people who knead people."

"Clones are people two."

"Pharmacists are the pill-ars of society."

Did you hear about the board carpenter?

Did you hear about the carpenter who was nailed for speeding?

13. NED & TED & OTHER EXCELLENT ADVENTURES

NACK: Why are you so mad?

NICK: I brought my leopard-skin coat to the cleaners.

NACK: What's wrong with that?

NICK: It came back spotless.

TED: I'm looking for square shoes.

NED: Why?

TED: Our house has a thousand square feet.

NAITER: Are you supposed to tip the waiters here?

WAITER: Yes.

NAITER: Good, because I've been waiting for twenty minutes.

HUBBY: I want to send my wife some clothes in the mail.

TUBBY: Why don't you?

HUBBY: I can't find her address.

HITTER: I'm depressed.

PITCHER: Why?

HITTER: I just had my tenth no-hitter.

PITCHER: That sounds good to me. Why are you depressed?

HITTER: I'm not a pitcher. I'm a boxer.

GLO: This sun tanning contest is only for amateurs.

FLO: How are they going to make sure there are no professionals?

GLO: All contestants will be screened.

JACK: I dropped my car off at the mechanic's this morning.

MACK: Did he give you a ride to work?

JACK: No, but he said he would take me to the cleaners.

NICK: How much for the fake beard?
RICK: Ten dollars, plus tax.
NICK: Forget the tax, I'll use glue.

LOU: My mail was damp this morning.
YOU: Maybe you had some postage dew.

WINK: I was at a hotel that was very exclusive.
LINK: How exclusive was it?
WINK: Room service had an unlisted number.

LINK: I couldn't find the elevator in my hotel.
WINK: Did you ask someone?
LINK: Yes, but you should have seen the stairs I
    got.

EVA: I was at a German restaurant last night.
IVY: How was it?
EVA: The appetizer was terrible and the wurst
    was yet to come.

Knock Knock.
    Who's there?
Sarasota.
    Sarasota who?
"Is Sar-a-soda in the house? I'm thirsty."

"I don't have a multiple personality,"
    Tom said, trying to be frank.

RED: Did you hear about the girl who ran for Queen of the blood donor clinic?

TED: No. What happened?

RED: She won Miss Congealeality.

PAT: I tried to turn my raincoat into a leather coat.

NAT: What happened?

PAT: Nothing. It couldn't be suede (swayed).

NOD: My radio is finally fixed.

TOD: You must be happy.

NOD: I'm ex-static.

DUFFY: You should never hit anyone with glasses.

TUFFY: I don't. I usually use a stick.

THOR: How do you like being a door?
DOOR: It's okay. People shouldn't knock it.

NED: Why are people throwing pennies at your
   pen?
TED: It's a fountain pen.

NICK: I couldn't find anyone in the shoe
   department.
NACK: No one?
NICK: Not a sole.

NED: How did you paint such a nice picture?
TED: Easel-y.

LOLO: They were planning to add my brother's head to Mount Rushmore.
POLO: What happened?
LOLO: They couldn't find rock that was thick enough.

SPOCK: How many ears do Trekkies have?
KLOCK: I don't know.
SPOCK: Three: A left ear, a right ear, and the final frontier.

FLIP: They have discovered an invisible universe.
FLOP: I just can't see it.

BILL: If you have a dime and a quarter, which one will jump off the bridge?
JILL: The dime might, but the quarter has more cents.

WON: My project on the stars came in second at the science fair.
TON: What did you win?
WON: The constellation prize.

LOU: How was the carnival?
SUE: Fair.

14. EAT YOUR HEART OUT

What do you say to an octopus at the dinner table?

"Get your elbow elbow elbow elbow elbow off the table."

What do you say to a liar at the dinner table?
"Pass the baloney."

What do you say to a politician at the dinner table?
"Pass the buck, please."

What is the orchestra's favorite food?
Cello (jello) pudding.

What is Big Foot's favorite food?
Sas-squash.

What is a radio announcer's favorite food?
Tune-a-sandwiches.

What is an Eskimo's favorite food?
Iceberg-ers (burgers).

What does a rich ham wear?
Designer cloves.

What do you call two morons drinking diet pop, eating apples and singing?
The Moron Tab-and-Apple Choir.

What did the scientist say when he found a 200-year-old sausage?
"I found the missing link."

What do you get when you cross a spaceship and a chef?
A flying sauce-r.

Serving Your Fellow Man

Why won't most cannibals eat clowns?
They taste funny.

Did you hear about the cannibal who was late for dinner?
They gave him the cold shoulder.

Did you hear about the cannibal who ate his mother-in-law?
She didn't agree with him.

Did you hear about the two cannibals who ordered "The Man From Prague?"
They decided to split the Czech.

Did you hear about the cannibal wedding reception?
They toasted the bride, and then they toasted the groom.

Why was the fat politician so happy about his weight?
He was gaining in the polls.

How do you cook an alligator?
In a crock pot.

Where do astronauts cook their food?
On a space wok (walk).

How do you catch celery?
You stalk it.

COOK: How did you weigh these fish?
KOOK: On a scale of one to ten.

Why can't two waiters play tennis?
They'll both want to serve.

Why were the apples and oranges all alone?
The banana split.

What does Charlie Brown like on his toast?
Peanuts butter.

What does a baby kangaroo have for breakfast?
Pouched (poached) eggs.

How did the comedian like his eggs?
Funny side up.

Did you hear about the smart cook?
He always used his noodle.

Why did the ice cream cone surrender?
He knew when he was licked.

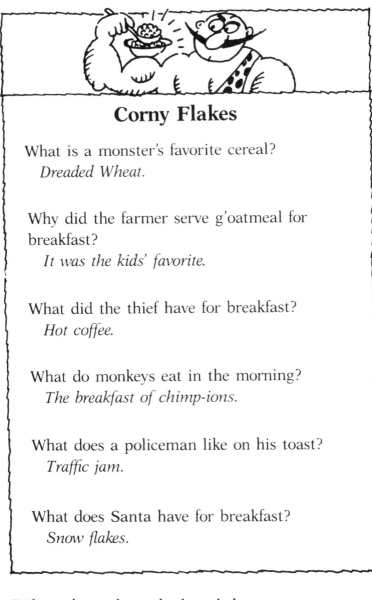

Corny Flakes

What is a monster's favorite cereal?
Dreaded Wheat.

Why did the farmer serve g'oatmeal for breakfast?
It was the kids' favorite.

What did the thief have for breakfast?
Hot coffee.

What do monkeys eat in the morning?
The breakfast of chimp-ions.

What does a policeman like on his toast?
Traffic jam.

What does Santa have for breakfast?
Snow flakes.

Did you hear about the bread that never went bad?
After they made it they broke the mold (mould).

What kind of shoes do bakers wear?
Loafers.

Why did the baker take a raisin out to a movie?
He didn't have a date.

Why did the baker quit making donuts?
He hated the hole business.

How much does Chinese soup weigh?
About won-ton (one ton).

What TV show do you watch after eating Chinese food?
Wheel of Fortune Cookies.

15. IS THERE A DOCTOR IN THE HOUSE?

ROCK: Doctor, hurry, I'm shrinking!
DOC: You'll just have to be a little patient.

DAC: Doctor, what would you take for a cold?
DOC: I'm not sure. Make me an offer.

Did you hear about the frustrated dietician?
His patience was wearing thin.

Where did the psychiatrist like to go for a walk?

Along the psychopath.

Why didn't the dentist ask his secretary on a date?

He was already taking out a tooth.

How did the dentist break his mirror?

Acci-dentally.

Where does the dentist get gas?

At the filling station.

What was the dentist doing in Panama?

Looking for the root canal.

What did the dentist see at the North Pole?
Molar Bears.

What does a dentist do on a roller coaster?
He braces himself.

What game did the dentist play as a child?
Caps and robbers.

What does The Dentist Of The Year get?
A little plaque.

Did you hear about the dentist who planted a garden?
A month later he was picking his teeth.

What did the undertaker say to the bill collector?
"I grave at the office."

Why did the TV producer go to the doctor?
To have his cast removed.

DAFFY: I just got my bill from my plastic surgeon.
LAFFY: A bill?
DAFFY: Yes. Next week I get my webbed feet.

LAFFY: Yesterday I had my appendix out.
DAFFY: Why?
LAFFY: My doctor was just making a little money on the side.

DOC: You'll never be happy 'til you get over these phobias.
TOC: I was afraid you'd say that.

What is a doctor's favorite musical instrument?
An ear drum.

Did you hear about the doctor who golfed in the dark?
He liked swinging nightclubs.

What was the doctor doing in the fridge?
Fixing a cold cut sandwich.

How did the psychologist change his flat?
With de-spair (the spare) tire.

Why did Zeus and Apollo hang out at the health club?
They were both myth-fits.

What did the man say after his knee operation?
"I stand corrected."

Why did the doctor get such a big dog?
He always wanted a lab assistant.

Why did the doctor return his dog to the pet store?
It wouldn't heel (heal).

What kind of mouthwash do doctors recommend?
Stetho-Scope.

How does a funeral home get rid of ashes?
The old fashioned way: They urn them.

LAD: How do I get to the morgue?
TAD: Turn left at the coroner.

Moaners and Groaners

What was the *Titanic* shivering for?
It was a nervous wreck.

What kind of person was the captain of the *Titanic*?
Deep down he was a nice guy.

What do you do when the road has a headache?
Ride on the shoulder.

What has no lungs or kidneys, but has thirteen hearts?
A deck of cards.

What did one casket say to the other casket?
"Is that you coffin (coughin')?"

Did you hear about the sad pillow?
It was a little down.

16. TUFF STUFF

Who fixes the president's teeth?
The presi-dentist.

What kind of shampoo does the president use?
Hair Force One.

Where does the president wipe his feet?
On a diplo-mat.

Where does the ambassador fish?
In the embass-sea (embassy).

How did the Congressman get a son?
He adopted a Bill.

What were the nylons doing in Washington, D.C.?

They were running for Congress.

How cold was it yesterday?

A politician had his hands in his own pockets.

Where does the British government keep its teacups?

In the Cabinet.

What did the king and queen of hearts do on their daughter's birthday?

They sent her a card.

Why should you be nice to moss?
For peat's sake.

Why was the aquarium depressed?
It lacked porpoise.

What is the worst part of snorkling?
It's a tank-less job.

What got the gutters in trouble?
Eaves dropping on the neighbors.

What got the house in trouble?
Siding with the neighbors.

What got the wall in trouble?
Being plastered.

What got the plywood in trouble?
Coming unglued.

Who do you take hunting for a frozen dinner?
A TV guide.

What happened when the plaid army met the striped army?
They clashed.

What do you get when you cross a lawyer with a tailor?

A suit case.

What do you get when you cross a math teacher with a tennis player?

A numbers racquet.

What do you get when you cross a taxidermist with a Big Mac?

Stuffed.

What do you call a sourpuss who watches too much TV?

A grouch potato.

What color do you always think you've seen before?

Deja-blue (déjà vu).

What is blue and a fake?
An artificial smurf.

What has twelve legs and two wings?
A hockey team.

What holds up the roof of a newspaper?
Gossip columns.

Famous Last Words

What did the oven cleaner always say?
"Grime doesn't pay."

What is the auto parts store slogan?
"You deserve a brake today."

What do you do if your skirt is too long?
Call the hem-line.

Who do you call if your bread is burnt?
Toastbusters.

What do you do if there is a flood?
Call the emerging-sea (emergency) number.

What did the dinosaur say when it started getting cold?
"I-ce shall return."

INDEX